Land and Water Combat Vehicles

Marie-Therese Miller

Lerner Publications ◆ Minneapolis

Thank you to all those who serve in the US military, with particular thanks to the Marine Corps and navy

Lerner Publications Company
An imprint of Lerner Publishing Group, Inc.
241 First Avenue North
Minneapolis, MN 55401 USA

For reading levels and more information, look up this title at www.lernerbooks.com.

Main body text set in Billy Infant Regular. Typeface provided by SparkType.

Editor: Cole Nelson

Library of Congress Cataloging-in-Publication Data

Names: Miller, Marie-Therese, author.
Title: Land and water combat vehicles / Marie-Therese Miller.
Description: Minneapolis : Lerner Publications, [2024] | Series: Lightning bolt books—Mighty military vehicles | Includes bibliographical references and index. | Audience: Ages 6–9 | Audience: Grades 2–3 | Summary: "How do marines get from ships to shore? Amphibious combat vehicles, or ACVs, do the job. ACVs sail on water and drive on land. Learn the history of ACVs and how they keep marines safe"— Provided by publisher.
Identifiers: LCCN 2023039253 (print) | LCCN 2023039254 (ebook) | ISBN 9798765626122 (library binding) | ISBN 9798765628980 (paperback) | ISBN 9798765635247 (epub)
Subjects: LCSH: Motor vehicles, Amphibious—United States—Juvenile literature
Classification: LCC V895 M55 2024 (print) | LCC V895 (ebook) | DDC 623.825—dc23/eng/20230825

LC record available at https://lccn.loc.gov/2023039253
LC ebook record available at https://lccn.loc.gov/2023039254

Manufactured in the United States of America
1-1009904-51946-10/16/2023

Table of Contents

From Sea to Shore

Amphibious combat vehicles (ACVs) get ready to leave the ship's well deck.

Their motors roar. The drivers close their hatches.

Marines board ACVs on land and at sea.

Each ACV holds up to sixteen marines. The vehicles drive from the well deck into the ocean. Then they sail away.

When the ACVs reach the shore, they drive onto the beach.

ACVs have both wheels to drive on land and propellers to sail at sea.

Marines often train in ACVs so they are ready whenever they need to set sail.

Some ACVs are personnel carriers. They protect and move marines from ship to shore and back again. They can sail the open ocean, bays, and rivers. ACVs can also drive across all kinds of land.

ACV Parts

ACVs are built for battle and to move marines safely. ACVs have eight wheels for land travel. They also have a powerful engine and two propellers.

The shape of an ACV's hull helps keep marines safe from explosions.

These vehicles have a hull shaped like a V. They also have special seats. Both hull and seats help protect marines from explosions.

Some ACVs have weapons on top. A common weapon is the machine gun.

The weapons on an ACV are placed near the top hatches.

ACVs have hatches toward the top. The driver can drive with the hatch open. Or the driver can close the hatch. Then they use cameras to see outside.

The US military uses two types of ACVs. The personnel ACV has an area where the marines sit.

There isn't much room in an ACV, but each one is full of high-tech equipment.

Marines use the computers and equipment in an ACV to see the battlefield and talk to other marines.

In the command and control ACV, that area might have computers. Marines use these computers to collect information and plan battles.

ACVs Then and Now

The military used amphibious assault vehicles to move marines in the 1970s.

These vehicles had tracks instead of wheels. They also had benches instead of seats.

Amphibious assault vehicles in the 1980s had tracks like a tank.

Marines started using ACVs in 2020. They can move more than 65 miles (105 km) per hour on land and 6 knots (6.9 miles, or 11 km) per hour over open ocean.

Navy ships launch ACVs. These ships sink a little so the well deck fills with water. The ACVs enter the ocean from the flooded well deck.

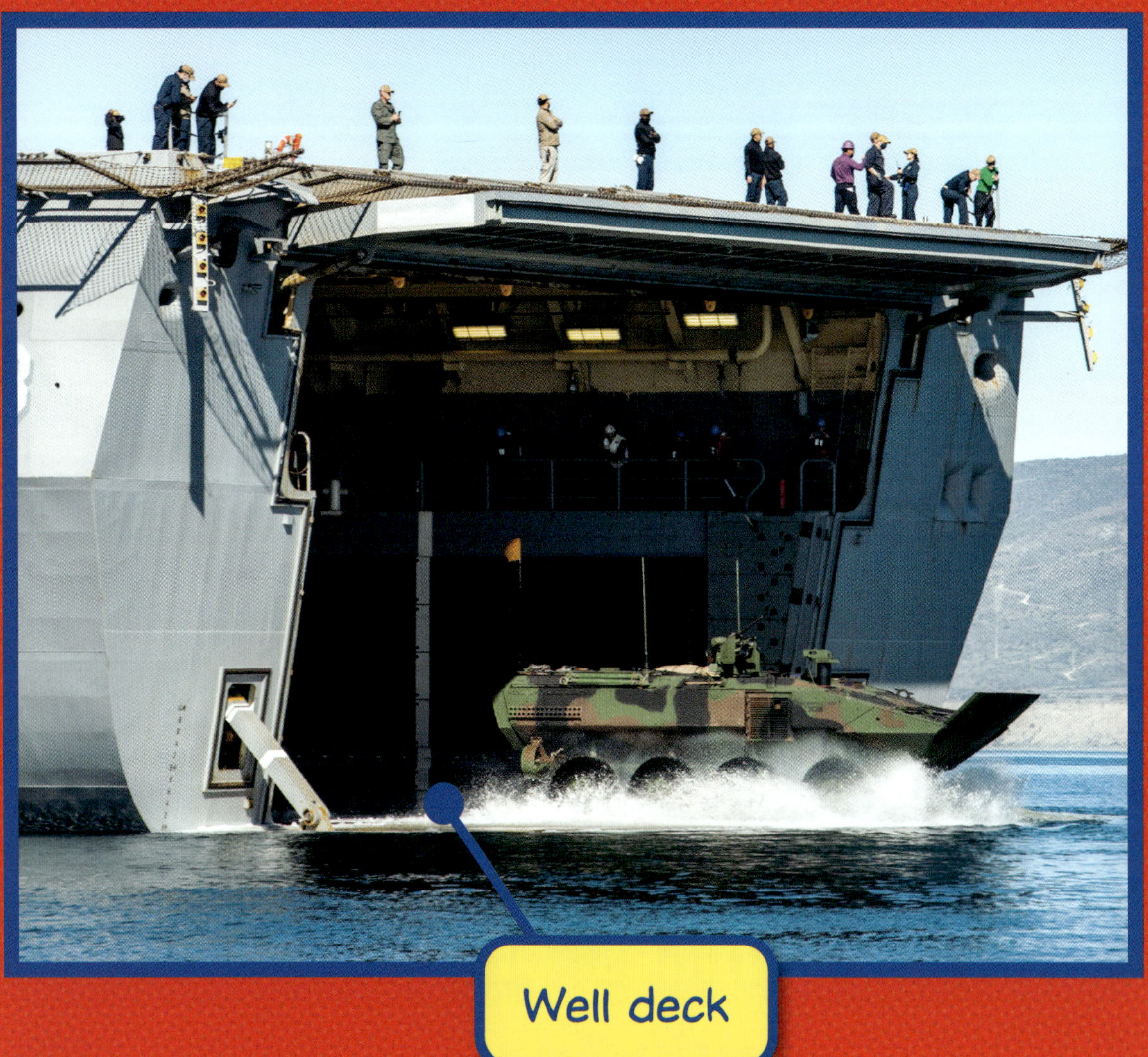

Well deck

One future kind of ACV will be able to fix other ACVs. It will also tow them away from danger. These will help keep marines safe on land and sea.

Vehicle Diagram

Amphibious Combat Vehicle

Fun Facts

- ACV drivers use regular cameras and cameras that detect heat to see.
- ACVs can travel during the day or night and in all kinds of weather.
- ACVs can be used to help in natural disasters, such as hurricanes.
- The US military also uses a hovercraft, called the landing craft air cushion (LCAC), to move soldiers and equipment from ship to beach.

Glossary

amphibious: used on both land and water

combat: fighting in a war

hatch: a small door or opening

hull: the body of a ship

personnel: people

tow: to pull along behind

Learn More

Britannica Kids: Marines
https://kids.britannica.com/kids/article/marines/353430

Britannica Kids: Navy
https://kids.britannica.com/kids/article/navy/353522

Garstecki, Julia. *US Marines*. Mankato, MN: Black Rabbit Books, 2021.

Kiddle: Naval Ship Facts for Kids
https://kids.kiddle.co/Naval_ship

London, Martha. *US Marine Corps Equipment and Vehicles*. Minneapolis: Kids Core, 2022.

Miller, Marie-Therese. *Strong Submarines*. Minneapolis: Lerner Publications, 2025.

Index

Photo Acknowledgments

Image credits: U.S. Marine Corps/Cpl. Laura Y. Raga, p. 4; U.S. Marine Corps/Cpl. Austin Gillam, p. 5; Cpl. U.S. Marine Corps/Jamin M. Powell, pp. 6, 20; U.S. Marine Corps/Lance Cpl. Willow Marshall, p. 7; U.S. Marine Corps/PO2 Hector Carrera, pp. 8, 18, 19; U.S. Marine Corps/2nd Lt. Joshua Estrada, p. 9; U.S. Marine Corps/Cpl. Cameron Hermanet, pp. 10, 12; U.S. Navy/Chief Mass Communication Specialist Michael Gomez, p. 11; U.S. Marine Corps/Sgt. Miguel A. Rosales, p. 13; U.S. Marine Corps/Sgt. Jailine L. AliceaSantiago, p. 14; AP Photo/Mell, p. 15; National Archives (330-CFD-DN-SN-83-05625), p. 16; U.S. Marine Corps/Lance Cpl. Drake Nickels, p. 17.

Cover: U.S. Marine Corps/PO2 Hector Carrera.